IELTS PRACTICE TESTS

Michael Garbutt & Kerry O'Sullivan

UPDATED EDITION

National Centre for English Language Teaching and Research

IELTS: Practice Tests
Updated edition

Published and distributed by the
National Centre for English
Language Teaching and Research
Macquarie University
Sydney NSW 2109

© Macquarie University 1991
Reprinted with corrections February 1995
Updated edition 1996
Reprinted 1998, 2000, 2001

Copyright

National Library of Australia Cataloguing-in-Publication data
Garbutt, Michael D
IELTS practice tests

Updated ed.
ISBN 1 86408 183 X

1. International English Language Testing System. 2. English Language – Textbooks for foreign speakers. 3. English Language – Examinations. I. Garbutt, Michael D. – IELTS. II. O'Sullivan, Kerry, 1952. III. National Centre for English Language Teaching and Research (Australia). IV. Title. V. Title: International English Language Testing System practice tests. VI. Title: IELTS.

428.34

The National Centre for English Language Teaching and Research (NCELTR) was established at Macquarie University in 1988. The National Centre forms part of the Linguistics Discipline within the School of Linguistics and Psychology at Macquarie University.

Printed by Ligare Pty Ltd, Riverwood NSW 2210
Cover design by Simon Leong Design

The authors take no responsibility for the factual accuracy of, or the views expressed in, reading passages in this book.

► CONTENTS

► INTRODUCTION

The purpose of this book is to help you practise for the International English Language Testing System (IELTS) test. By doing these practice tests, you will:

- ◢ Become more familiar with the format of the IELTS test
- ◢ Understand the importance of time-management in successfully completing an IELTS test
- ◢ become more aware of your areas of difficulty in the IELTS test.

There is generally a break between the writing and speaking sections.

Each of the sections contains a variety of tasks designed to test your English-language proficiency. Although the range of tasks will vary from test to test, the strategies presented in this book are intended to develop a level of English-language proficiency which will enable you to deal with a wide range of different task types.

It is important to note that there are two different types of test. If you are planning to study at university you will be required to take the **IELTS Academic Module**. If you are planning to undertake a non-tertiary course or non-degree training you will be required to take the **IELTS General Training Module**. The format of both modules is identical but the reading passages and writing tasks in the General Training Module do not reflect tertiary study requirements.

The **General Training Module** is designed for students who intend to enter non-tertiary or non-degree courses. The format of this module is identical to the Academic Module, but the reading passages and writing tasks do not reflect tertiary study requirements. General Training Module candidates take the same Listening and Speaking sections as other candidates. If you intend to take the General Training Module, you should pay particular attention to the General Training Module Practice Test on page 45.

Using this book

We recommend that you do the Practice Tests under test conditions. You should not use dictionaries or any other resources. You should also make sure that you adhere to the time limits stated throughout each test.

After completing each Practice Test, check your answers against those provided in the Answer Keys (page 71). You need to identify those areas which have caused you difficulty and focus on these in your test preparation. To help you develop a more effective test preparation program, you may find it useful to consult *IELTS Strategies for Study*, which offers a comprehensive guide to test preparation.

Good luck with your studies.

Kerry O'Sullivan
Michael Garbutt

▶ PRACTICE TEST 1
Academic Module

All answers must be written on the answer sheet.

The test is divided as follows:

- ◢ Reading Passage 1   *Questions 1–10*
- ◢ Reading Passage 2   *Questions 11–16*
- ◢ Reading Passage 3   *Questions 17–23*

Start at the beginning of the test and work through it. You should answer all the questions. If you cannot do a particular question leave it and go on the next one. You can return to it later.

TIME ALLOWED: Reading   *60 minutes*

SECTION 1: READING

PART 1: EARTHQUAKE PREDICTION

You should spend about 15 minutes on Questions 1–10.

Questions 1– 4

Answer these questions by referring to **Reading Passage 1: Earthquake Prediction**.

1. Scientists attempt to find out three things about earthquakes. What are they?

   A. ....

   B. ....

   C. ....

2. 'The electrical and magnetic properties of crustal rocks are particularly sensitive to strain, and studies measuring changes which occur in these properties have provided promising results.' (Paragraph 5.) What is the function of this sentence? Choose one of the functions listed below, and write A, B, C or D in the space provided.

   A. to provide an example of a previous idea

   B. to summarise the paragraph

   C. to provide an argument against the previous idea

   D. to establish the main point of the passage.

Your answer: ....

3. The passage describes two phenomena observed in animals prior to earthquakes.
   What are they?

   A. ....   B. ....

4. According to paragraph 5, measuring the conductivity of fluid in rock may not be a reliable earthquake predictor, because:

A. other factors may account for changes in conductivity

B. rock may be saturated with fluid

C. these changes can be measured

D. the conductivity of crustal rock is inherently variable

Your answer: ....

READING PASSAGE 1: EARTHQUAKE PREDICTION

Since antiquity, the devastating effects of earthquakes on human lives and property have encouraged the search for reliable methods of earthquake prediction. This challenge remains and contemporary seismologists continue to seek reliable methods for pinpointing the time, place and magnitude of individual quakes.

One prediction technique involves an analysis of the recurrence rates of earthquakes as indicators of future seismic activity. Earthquakes are concentrated in certain areas of the world where tectonic plates such as the Pacific Plate, the Eurasian Plate and the African Plate meet and create fault zones and it is in these areas that seismologists focus their investigations.

The plate tectonics model provides another tool for earthquake prediction by calculating the accumulated strain at plate boundaries. When the strain reaches a certain magnitude the pressure must be released and it is therefore hypothesised that in such cases an earthquake is imminent.

The search for premonitory phenomena has received particular attention. In contrast to the ancient Greeks and Romans, who relied on the howling of dogs as a warning sign, modern seismologists have focused on physical evidence for an impending earthquake. Evidence of plate strain can be found by measuring relative movements in geodetic stations, while chemical changes also offer signals for seismologists. Using chemical-detection techniques, Professor Ulomov established a link between the rise in the concentration of radon gas in mineral water in the Tashkent Basin and the subsequent earthquake in 1966.

Analysis of the changes in magnetic properties and conductivity of rocks provides further data for prediction. The electrical and magnetic properties of crustal rocks are particularly sensitive to strain and studies measuring changes which occur in these properties have provided promising results. The conductivity of crustal rock is determined by the degree to which the rock is saturated with fluid and the electrolytic properties of those fluids. Before large earthquakes, small fractures develop in rocks, which changes the quantity of fluid present. These changes can be measured and provide useful predictive data. However, similar changes in the fluid-bearing capacity of rock can occur as a result of other factors such as changes in the water table, and therefore this technique is not entirely reliable.

The ancient belief that the behaviour of birds, cats and dogs provides evidence of imminent earthquakes has recently gained credence as a result of tests carried out in

California. It has been shown that changes take place in the metabolic rates of these animals which correlate with subsequent seismic activity. It is hypothesised that the animals are sensitive to the seismic waves which precede major quakes.

In zones where earthquakes are known to occur, improved construction techniques can significantly reduce the effects of seismic waves. If more accurate information regarding the time and magnitude were available, governments could take even more effective measures to reduce the impact on human life. If, however, an entirely accurate prediction technique became available, there would be significant social and political implications. An earthquake prediction in a major urban area, for example, would require governments to provide an effective evacuation strategy, necessitating massive resourcing and political will.

Questions 5–10

By referring to Reading Passage 1, decide whether the following statements are true or false. Tick either True or False in the boxes provided.

	TRUE	FALSE
5. The search for reliable methods of earthquake prediction has been prompted by the devastating effects of earthquakes.	☐	☐
6. Seismologists are able to predict earthquakes entirely accurately.	☐	☐
7. Earthquakes only occur in the Pacific, Eurasian, and African Plates.	☐	☐
8. Earthquakes are caused by the plate tectonics model.	☐	☐
9. An increase in the level of radon gas in water always indicates an imminent earthquake.	☐	☐
10. Animal metabolisms are affected by seismic waves.	☐	☐

PART 2: THE MASSA DAM DISASTER

You should spend about 15 minutes on Questions 11–16.

Answer these questions by referring to Reading Passage 2: The Massa Dam Disaster. Choose the correct answer and write the appropriate letter in the space provided.

Questions 11–16

example: According to the passage, major construction projects:

    A. result in unforeseen and disastrous consequences

    B. may lead to unforeseen and disastrous consequences

    C. do not impact on geological features

    D. existing geological features impact on major construction projects.

Your answer: ..B..

11. The 250 metre-high wave was caused by:
    A. a compressed-air blast
    B. a rockslide
    C. the failure of control systems
    D. the collapse of high-level bridges

12. The 1 April landslide involved approximately:
    A. 500,000 cubic metres of rock
    B. 5,000,000 cubic metres of rock and water
    C. 180,000,000 cubic metres of material
    D. 250,000,000 cubic metres of water

13. Between the dam's completion and its collapse the site showed:
    A. no evidence of slippage
    B. a constant rate of slippage
    C. a decreasing rate of slippage
    D. an accelerating rate of slippage

14. At the time of the disaster, the elevation of the reservoir was:
    A. 590 metres   B. 500 metres   C. 495 metres   D. 475 metres

15. The Massa commission of enquiry recommended that:
    A. accurate geological surveys should be carried out before dam construction.
    B. abutment sizes should be doubled.
    C. the rate of acceleration from creep to landslide can be very rapid.
    D. more drastic reductions in reservoir elevations should be made in the event of an imminent collapse.

16. The passage suggests that responsibility for the disaster is attributable to:
    A. Dr. Magnus Krool
    B. Chief Engineer Pulsaar
    C. Both Krool and Pulsaar
    D. Dr Ruiq
    E. All of the above.

Your answers:

11. ....   13. ....   15. ....
12. ....   14. ....   16. ....

READING PASSAGE 2: THE MASSA DAM DISASTER

The impact of major construction projects on existing geological features may result in unforeseen and disastrous consequences.

This is illustrated by one of the worst dam disasters in history which occurred at the Massa Dam on 1 April 1958 only two years after the dam had opened to international acclaim as one of the great engineering achievements of the 20th century. Designed to supply electricity for the region's developing industrial sector and irrigation for the farmers of the arid Lower Massa Basin, the Massa project had taken seven years to complete. It took only seven minutes to collapse as an enormous landslide consisting of over 180 million cubic metres of rock tumbled down the right bank and fell into the reservoir behind the dam wall. The landslide created a 250 metre-high wave preceded by a compressed-air blast which entered the interior workings of the dam, smashed the wall abutments and destroyed all control systems. As the wave poured down the valley, it swept away three high-level bridges and obliterated the town of Sesai, killing its 1000 inhabitants. The wave was still 50 metres high when it reached the Kere River over two kilometres away.

The Massa disaster bore a striking resemblance to the Ryshkyk tragedy of 1949 when 500 people had been killed by a wall of water which had overtopped the dam abutments following a 100,000,000 cubic metre landslide. Both the Massa and Ryshkyk dam locations presented similar geological features: young folded limestone mountains with steeply tilted slopes offering no resistance to gravity sliding.

The commission of enquiry set up to investigate the causes of the Massa disaster heard that although Wolf Mason, the building contractors, had been aware of the findings of the investigations carried out after Ryshkyk they had disregarded two recommendations made by the Ryshkyk commission of enquiry's report. The report had concluded that the Ryshkyk design engineers had been foolhardy to locate the dam in an area of permeable rock characterised by fractures. The Ryshkyk report also noted that the abutment measurements—a height of 20 metres above maximum reservoir elevation, and a thickness of 10 metres—should have been doubled.

At the Massa enquiry, Wolf Mason's engineer, Dr H. L. Ruiq, claimed that the presence of 50-metre deep clay marls underlying the limestone at Massa invalidated the relevance of the Ryshkyk recommendations, while the increased height and width of the Massa abutments, though not double those recommended by the Ryshkyk enquiry, were sufficient for the lower maximum reservoir elevation existing at Massa. The Massa site, he added, had been thoroughly surveyed and provided no evidence for the presence of dangerous levels of slippage. In its final report, the Massa Commission accepted Dr Ruiq's evidence and cleared him of responsibility for the disaster.

The events which preceded the fatal 1 April movement, however, suggest that it was not as unpredictable as those involved in the dam's management claimed at the enquiry. Minor landslides had been common in the upper Massa valley even before the construction of the dam. After the construction of the dam and the flooding of the valley behind it, geologists found a 30-metre rise in the level of ground water surrounding the reservoir. Fractures in the permeable limestone further increased the hydrostatic uplift and this resulted in an increase of the observed land creep from an average of one centimetre per month registered in June 1956 to one centimetre per week by December of that year. This phenomenon resulted in an increase in the frequency and size of landslides, leading to a slide of 500,000 cubic metres on the right bank near the dam wall at the beginning of January.

In response to this, the chief engineer, Lennart Pulsaar, ordered a reduction in the eleva-tion of the reservoir from 590 metres to 500 metres. In addition, a network of geodetic stations was installed to measure any movement in the potential slide area. They record-ed a slope creep of one centimetre per week. The area was also explored by drill holes in a search for a major slide plane. No such plane was detected and Pulsaar submitted a report which claimed that landslides of a greater magnitude than 1,000,000 cubic metres were unlikely to occur and that the reduction in reservoir capacity was sufficient to accommodate up to 5,000,000 cubic metres of material.

The commission of enquiry found that the drill holes made by Pulsaar's team were too shallow to intercept the major slide plane which led to the subsequent disaster.

The rains which fell throughout March 1956 caused heavy run-off, which further raised the level of hydrostatic pressure. In addition, despite the reduction in the level of storage capacity, maximum lateral infiltration resulting from the previously higher level did not peak until about late March. By early March, the geodetic sensors were recording a slope creep of one centimetre per day.

At this time, some geodetic stations were observed to be moving at one centimetre per day. The chief geologist at the site, Dr Magnus Krool, who analysed the data, believed that the stations were moving in blocks and did not suspect that the entire area was moving as a single mass. When it was realised on 31 March that the right bank was in fact moving as a single mass at a rate of eight centimetres per day, the elevation of the reservoir was lowered a further 25 metres as a precautionary measure. The effects of this action, however, were reduced by a heavy inflow from run-off. When the landslide occurred the next day, the effective level of the reservoir was only five metres lower than it had been.

The commission of enquiry concluded that, despite accurate geological surveys of dam sites before construction, rock masses under changed environmental conditions as a result of dam construction can be subject to significant weakening in a very short time and that the rate of acceleration from creep to collapse can occur in a matter of days. It therefore recommended the use of more accurate systems for observing and measuring changes in a rock mass and the adoption of more drastic reductions in reservoir elevations if a collapse appeared imminent.

Glossary:

abutment: part of a dam wall

creep: slow, downward movement

elevation: height

PART 3: THE GOLDWATER GATE BRIDGE COLLAPSE

You should spend about 30 minutes on Questions 17–36.

Reading Passage 3 describes a problem in the construction of span 5 of the Goldwater Gate Bridge and presents the six stages of the solution to this problem. By referring to the reading passage, match the phrases A–H listed below with questions 17–22. Note that there are more phrases than are necessary. The first one has been done for you as an example.

Questions 17–22   *Your answers:*

example:

    Problem in Span 5   *A*
                                 ....

17. Solution, stage one   ....

18. Solution, stage two   ....

19. Solution, stage three   ....

20. Solution, stage four   ....

21. Solution, stage five   ....

22. Solution, stage six   ....

A. some boxes were buckled.

B. stiffening members were inserted into the sagging half-span.

C. more boxes were cantilevered out to weigh down the damaged half-span.

D. damaged bolts were removed from the buckled half-span.

E. work proceeded on the construction of span 4.

F. the buckled half-span was aligned with and joined to the strengthened half-span.

G. new bolts were inserted in the damaged section.

H. steel beams were added to strengthen the second half-span.

I. the spans were divided into smaller sections.

These questions deal with the construction of the central span. Match the phrases A–F listed below with questions 23–27. Note that there are more phrases than are necessary.

Your answers:

23. Initial problem   ....

24. Attempted solution   ....

25. Unexpected result   ....

26. Action taken   ....

27. Final result   ....

A. the use of 80 tons of kentledge
B. addition of cantilevered boxes
C. bolts were removed from the buckled half-span
D. a difference in levels between the half-spans as a result of buckling
E. collapse of span
F. more extensive buckling developed

READING PASSAGE 3: THE GOLDWATER GATE BRIDGE COLLAPSE

Construction of the Goldwater Gate Bridge, designed to provide the city of Kersal with a first and much-needed link across the Irwell River, began in 1978 and was scheduled for completion in late 1980 at a cost of $60 million. By February 1980, as a result of labour disputes and technical difficulties, the contractors, International Constructions Ltd., were forced to reschedule the completion date for early 1981, estimating final costs at $96 million. In reality, the bridge would not be completed until 1988 at a cost of $500 million and 18 lives.

The project involved the construction of two concrete approach viaducts on each bank of the Irwell linked by a central 800 metre central steel section. The steel section was to be composed of five spans supported by six concrete piers. Steel cables running from cable towers on the two central piers would link the longest central span to the adjoining spans.

After the construction of the concrete viaducts, the central steel section of the bridge was built using the 'box-girder' construction technique. As each of the spans weighed around 1000 tonnes they were divided into smaller sections known as box-girder units, each weighing around 110 tonnes. The box girders were assembled on the ground to form two longitudinal half-spans which could then be lifted separately to lighten the load.

In the next stage, one longitudinal half-span was lifted up, placed on roller beams resting on a temporary wooden pier and levered into position on the concrete pier. The

GOLDWATER GATE BRIDGE

second half-span was lifted in the same way from the other side of the pier and joined to the first half-span.

Difficulties arose, however, in April 1981, during the construction of span 5. When the first half-span was about to be rolled from its temporary pier onto the concrete pier, engineers discovered that some of the boxes had buckled by up to 475 millimetres.

This would have resulted in an unacceptable difference of 100 millimetres between the surface levels of the half-span and the second half-span to be installed on the other side. The engineers took the decision to proceed and located the damaged half-span in place on the concrete pier. The second half-span was then strengthened by the addition of steel beams to avoid similar buckling and also lifted into position. The slightly lower buckled half-span was jacked up until the two sections were in vertical alignment and then joined.

An attempt was then made to rectify the buckling in the damaged half-span by inserting 250 millimetre steel beams as stiffening members. Although this removed most of the initial sag it was found that a section in the middle of the span could not be straightened by this method. In response to this situation, further boxes were added to the span by the cantilever process. It was hoped that their added weight would reduce sagging in the buckled area. The engineers removed the damaged bolts from an inner girder in the halfspan in an attempt to provide greater flexibility. The operation was successful and the sag disappeared. The damaged bolts were replaced and work proceeded on the construction of span 4.

A similar problem was encountered during the construction of the final central section. When the two longitudinal half-spans were brought together, there was an eight centimetre difference between the height of the two half-spans. The engineers decided to use 'kentledge' or weighting to solve the problem. This involved placing 80 tonnes of concrete on the higher half-span in an attempt to force it down. After placing the final concrete block on the half-span, however, a buckle appeared in it which was even larger than the one which had been found earlier. The two half-spans were still on their temporary bearings and it was not therefore possible to add further cantilevered boxes as had been done before.

In order to provide flexibility, it was decided to remove bolts in groups of six or eight in the section of the half-span where the buckling was greatest. After the removal of 30 bolts the bulge began to subside. At this point, however, a buckle appeared in both the half-spans. The weight of the whole eastern half-span was now supported only by the western half-span. Slowly, but inexorably, the eastern half-span slipped at an increasingly acute angle before plunging 150 metres to the mud flats in the Irwell River below. Of the 36 men working on it, 18 were killed and another 16 seriously injured. In a report issued by the commission of enquiry, responsibility was attributed to a combination of a flawed design, an impractical assembly technique and a rash corrective intervention which had been compounded by inadequately observed safety procedures.

Glossary:

bolt: a metal pin

buckle: bend under pressure

sag: curve downwards

bulge: swell upwards

Questions 28–36

The following passage summarises the events which preceded the fatal collapse of the central span of the Goldwater Gate Bridge. Match the phrases A – P with the gaps in the summary and write your answers in the space provided. (There are more phrases than gaps provided.) The first one has been done for you as an example.

A. both half-spans	I. placing 80 tonnes of concrete
B. the required flexibility	J. the greatest degree of buckling
C. to rectify the buckling	K. the previously successful
D. bringing together	L. 30 bolts
E. to increase the sag	M. resting on concrete piers
F. the unstable	N. further extensive buckling of the damaged half-span
G. the span's position on temporary bearings	O. the provision of flexibility
H. the difference in elevations between the two half-spans	P. discovered by engineers

After ...(example)... the two half-spans it was ...28... that one half-span was higher than the other. In order to eliminate ...29... kentledge was employed. This, however, resulted in ...30... and the need to adopt new measures.

As a result of the ...31..., the solution used for span five was unworkable. Unable to employ ...32... cantilevered box system, the engineers were forced to find an alternative method ...33... .

It was hoped to achieve ...34... by removing bolts in that section of the half-span which exhibited ...35... . As a consequence of the removal of ...36..., one half-span collapsed, killing 18 men.

Your answers:

example: ...D...

28. ...P...   31. ....   34. ....

29. ....   32. ....   35. ....

30. ....   33. ....   36. ....

SECTION 2: WRITING

Writing Task 1

You should spend a maximum of 20 minutes on this task.

The safe and effective disposal of domestic and industrial wastes plays an important role in pollution control. The diagram below shows how liquid domestic and industrial wastes are recycled.

As a class assignment you have to write a description of how pure water is obtained from polluted domestic and industrial sources.

TASK: Based on the information in the diagram below, write a minimum of 100 words describing the process and the equipment required. If you wish, you may also use your own knowledge and experience. Your description must be relevant to the question.

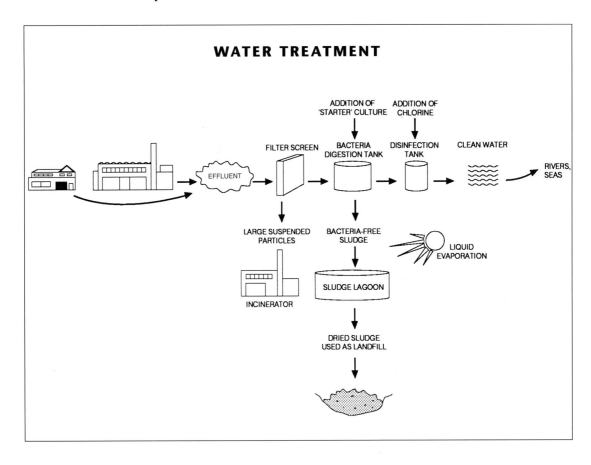

WATER TREATMENT

Writing Task 1. Write your answer here.

Writing Task 2

You should spend about 40 minutes on this task.

Following the Chernobyl nuclear disaster it has become increasingly obvious that nuclear reactors constitute a potentially devastating threat to human and environmental health.

Should governments continue to maintain and develop nuclear power plants? What are the risks and benefits associated with nuclear power production?

You should write a minimum of 250 words.

You should use your own ideas, knowledge and experience and support your arguments with examples and relevant evidence.

NOTES

Writing Task 2. Write your answer here.

_____

_____

_____

_____

_____

_____

_____

_____

_____

_____

_____

_____

_____

_____

_____

_____

_____

_____

_____

_____

_____

_____

_____

_____

_____

_____

_____

_____

_____

_____

_____

_____

▶ PRACTICE TEST 2
Academic Module

All answers must be written on the answer sheet.

The test is divided as follows:

◢	Reading Passage 1	*Questions 1–10*
◢	Reading Passage 2	*Questions 11–16*
◢	Reading Passage 3	*Questions 17–23*

Start at the beginning of the test and work through it. You should answer all the questions. If you cannot do a particular question leave it and go on to the next one. You can return to it later.

SECTION 1: READING

Part 1: Systemic Poisons
You should spend about 15 minutes on Questions 1–9.

Question 1

Paragraph 1 of Reading Passage 1 refers to three metals. What are they?

1. A. ....

   B. ....

   C. ....

According to Reading Passage 1, decide whether the following statements are true or false. Tick either True or False in the boxes provided.

	TRUE	FALSE
2. 'Villi' are capillary blood vessels.	☐	☐
3. The intestinal section is located between the villi and the stomach.	☐	☐
4. Lead poisoning affects the gastrointestinal tract.	☐	☐
5. The ingestion of non-soluble poisons may cause vomiting.	☐	☐

Questions 6-8

By referring to Reading Passage 1, match the phrases A to I below with the descriptions numbered 6 to 8. Write your answers in the spaces provided. Write only one letter in each space. Note that there are more phrases than you will need.

A. mucous-producing glands
B. transportation and industry
C. penetration of stomata
D. ingestion
E. root system absorption

F. damage to central nervous system
G. upper-bowel tract
H. villi
I. rainfall

Your answers:

6. Source of systemic poisons ....

7. Method of entry into humans ....

8. One effect of poisoning ....

Question 9

Paragraph 2 of Reading Passage 1 describes two ways in which poisons are absorbed by plant tissues. According to the information in this paragraph, which two of the following describe these ways?

A. absorption through root system
B. contamination by vegetable matter
C. poisons land in soils
D. entry through leaves
E. gravity and rainfall

Your answer:

9. ....

READING PASSAGE 1: HEALTH EFFECTS OF SYSTEMIC POISONS

Although the detrimental effects of systemic poisons such as lead have been known for many years, it is only recently that cadmium and mercury have been recognised as equally damaging toxic agents. The absorption of such metal toxins via the food chain is a common means of poisoning.

After emission from industrial smokestacks or car exhausts, gravity and rainfall return the toxin-containing pollutants to earth. They may then be absorbed by plants in two possible ways. Where metal poisons have landed in the surrounding soil, the plant's root system absorbs them and distributes them throughout the plant's tissues. Toxins may also fall directly onto leaves and enter through stomata on the leaves. When vegetable matter has been contaminated in this way and is subsequently ingested by humans or animals, the gastrointestinal tract becomes the main pathway for the toxins' entry into the bloodstream.

The intestinal section located between the upper-bowel tract and the stomach is lined with many finger-like projections of mucous membrane, known as 'villi'. The villi are surrounded by capillary blood vessels, whose function is to absorb the products of digestion. Soluble poisons are rapidly absorbed by the villi into the bloodstream. In the case of lead poisoning, this results in a wide variety of effects on the blood-forming mechanism, the gastrointestinal tract and the central nervous system.

The passage of non-soluble poisons through the digestive system stimulates mucous-producing glands in the stomach and bowel. The production of mucous then induces spastic movements of the stomach which may result in the expulsion of the toxins by vomiting or as fecal matter via the lower intestine. The ingestion of non-soluble toxins is associated with fecal blood, diarrhoea and constipation.

PART 2: ASBESTOS

You should spend about 15 minutes on Questions 10–25.

Questions 10–25

The passage below summarises the main points of Reading Passage 2. Decide which word or phrase should go in each gap and write the corresponding letter in the space provided. Write only one letter in each space.

Summary of 'Asbestos Inhalation'

Due to its ___example___, asbestos has been __10__ since ancient times in a wide range of __11__. When asbestos __12__ are __13__ they pass through a series of __14__ which arrest their __15__. The stimulation of __16__ causes __17__ which expels them from the respiratory tract. If particles are very __18__, which is the case with __19__ asbestos, they may __20__ as far as the alveoli. Some of these particles may __21__ the alveolar wall and cause __22__ to develop. This reduces the __23__ of the lung and causes the condition known as __24__. Symptoms of the disease may take up to __25__ to appear.

A. coughing	F. extend	K. mucous lining	P. 30 years
B. versatility	G. 20 years	L. small	Q. particles
C. reach	H. applications	M. penetrate	R. used
D. asbestosis	I. smaller	N. efficiency	S. blue
E. scarring	J. filters	O. inhaled	T. progress

Your answers:

example: B.................................

10.	14............................	18............................	22. ....
11.	15............................	19............................	23. ....
12.	16............................	20............................	24. ....
13.	17............................	21............................	25. ....

READING PASSAGE 2: ASBESTOS INHALATION

Asbestos is the generic name for a number of naturally occurring fibrous mineral silicates of which the most common types are crocidolite, also known as blue asbestos, and chrysotile (white asbestos).

Employed for at least 2000 years, it is valued by industry because of its tensile strength and flexibility, and its resistance to acids, heat and friction. Asbestos has had a very wide variety of applications. It has been commonly employed in the building industry as a fireproofing agent and as a strengthener. The metal frames of buildings were sprayed with an asbestos solution to prevent the spread of fires, while asbestos was routinely mixed in with cement to provide greater resistance to weathering agents. It is also used in motor-vehicle brake linings, gas-mask filters, certain types of talcum powder, fire-resistant clothing, corrugated-iron roofing and in water and air pipes. As a result of such wide employment, it is likely that most people have been exposed to at least a small quantity of asbestos fibres.

During inhalation, all particles which enter the respiratory tract pass through a series of filter mechanisms. Particles are filtered out at different points of the respiratory tract depending on their size. The smaller the particle, the further into the respiratory it may penetrate before being arrested. The first set of filters consists of the hairs and mucous lining of the nose and mouth which prevent the entry of larger particles. When large particles are inhaled, they stimulate this mucous lining, which results in coughing and the consequent expulsion of the particles. The mucous lining extends downwards through hair-lined bronchial tubes of increasingly fine diameter which further filter the air before it reaches the respiratory bronchioles, a series of very fine tubes attached to air exchange chambers known as alveoli. The alveoli are composed of a thin layer of cells through which oxygen passes into blood vessels and is then distributed to the bloodstream.

Particles smaller than eight micrometres may reach the alveoli. This is the case with blue asbestos particles, which are very straight and slender and tend not to be arrested by mucous and expelled. As a result, they may reach the alveoli and penetrate the delicate cells lining the walls.

Some asbestos fibrils (particles) which reach the alveoli may be surrounded by scavenger cells known as macrophages, which serve to remove the fibrils from the body by expectoration or excretion. Other particles may remain in the alveoli with no adverse effects In cases where the asbestos particles have penetrated the alveolar wall, scar tissue develops. This reduces the effectiveness of the alveoli and so less oxygen passes into the blood and less carbon dioxide is removed from it. This condition is known as asbestosis. The process of scarring may take place gradually and the disease may not be diagnosed until 20 or 30 years after the initial exposure.

PART 3: ASBESTOS-RELATED DISEASES

You should spend about 15 minutes on Questions 26–30.

Questions 26–30

Five phrases have been left out of Reading Passage 3 'Asbestos-related Diseases' on page 170. Decide which phrase from the list A–H should go in each gap and write the letter in the space provided. The first one has been done for you as an example.

A. the incidence of mesothelioma is extremely low

B. which may extend from 25 to 30 years after initial exposure

C. whereas the latter consist of a collection of fluid in the chest region outside the lungs

D. on the other hand, is exclusively associated with exposure to the less harmful white asbestos

E. such as asbestosis and lung cancer

F. causing scarring which limits the functioning of the lungs

G. resulting from inadequate ventilation

H. develop the barrel-shaped chests associated with emphysema, cyanosis, (where the skin assumes a bluish colour) and club fingers

Your answers:

example: ..E...

26...

27...

28...

29...

30...

READING PASSAGE 3: ASBESTOS-RELATED DISEASES

The inhalation of asbestos particles is associated with a number of lung diseases
(example) .

Asbestosis is caused by the entry of asbestos particles into the walls of the alveoli, __26__ .
The lung loses its elasticity and may change shape. The initial symptoms of asbestosis
are a tightness in the chest and breathlessness. In its later stages, sufferers __27__ .

Lung cancer, the generic term for malignant tumours of the alveoli and bronchial tubes,
has been shown to be directly related to the inhalation of asbestos particles. As in the
case of asbestosis, there is generally a period of latency __28__ , despite the absence of
further exposure. Research suggests that there is a direct correlation between the degree
of exposure to asbestos and the incidence of lung cancers. Where exposure occurs, the
level of risk is further increased by cigarette smoking. Asbestos workers who smoke cig-
arettes have a 90% greater risk of contracting lung cancer than workers who do not
smoke.

Exposure to blue asbestos has been shown to produce mesothelioma, a rare cancer of
the outer lining of the lung or pleura. In a normal population __29__ . Where epidemio-
logical surveys have revealed a higher incidence of the disease, it is almost always
related to asbestos exposure.

Other changes in lung tissue caused by exposure to asbestos are pleural plaques and
effusions. The former refer to a thickening of the lining of the chest wall, __30__ . Pleural
plaques commonly remain undiagnosed and generally have no detrimental effect on
health.

PART 4: SAFETY RECOMMENDATIONS

You should spend about 20 minutes on Questions 31–36.

Questions 31–36

Answer the following questions by referring to Reading Passage 4. For each question
choose one answer and write the corresponding letter in the space provided. The first
one has been done for you as an example.

example:

According to paragraph 1, the commission of enquiry was instituted as a result of:

A. medical reports of asbestos-related deaths.

B. pressure from the building industry.

C. public apprehension concerning the effects of asbestos.

D. the health hazards associated with the use of asbestos in the building industry.

31. According to paragraph 2:

    A. exposure to even minimal levels of asbestos is unacceptable.

    B. asbestos should not be used in the building industry.

    C. the findings of US and Canadian reports differed from the NMRC report.

    D. the characteristics of asbestos would probably assure its future use.

32. The report assumed that asbestos would continue to be employed in the building industry on the basis of evidence provided by:

    A. its versatility and cost effectiveness.

    B. building workers.

    C. building management and economists.

    D. US and Canadian reports.

    E. none of the above.

33. In bonded form:

    A. no asbestos fibres are released.

    B. asbestos fibres may enter the air.

    C. there is an increased likelihood that asbestos fibres enter the air.

    D. asbestos can be bonded with cement.

34. Dust formation can be reduced by:

    A. the use of wetted, bonded forms of asbestos.

    B. inadequate ventilation.

    C. the use of protective respiratory equipment.

    D. the vacuuming of clothing.

35. The report claimed that:

    A. higher levels of amosite and chrysotile can be safely inhaled.

    B. lower levels of amosite and chrysotile are dangerous.

    C. white asbestos can be safely inhaled only in smaller quantities than blue asbestos.

    D. there are no safe maximum levels of asbestos inhalation.

36. The statement that 'If [maximum exposure levels] are strictly adhered to, the onset of asbestosis in a normal working life should not develop' is:

    A. the opinion of the writer of the reading passage.

    B. a claim made by the authors of the NMRC report.

    C. the assurance given by critics of the report.

    D. a claim rejected by building workers.

Your answers:

example: .C.....................................

31. .... 33. .... 35. ....

32. .... 34. .... 36. ....

READING PASSAGE 4: SAFETY RECOMMENDATIONS

In 1967, in response to widespread public concern aroused by medical reports of asbestos-related deaths, the National Medical Research Council instituted a commission of enquiry to investigate the health hazards associated with the use of asbestos in the building industry.

After examining evidence submitted by medical researchers and representatives of building workers and management, the NMRC published a report which included guidelines for handling asbestos. The report confirmed the findings of similar research in the United States and Canada. Exposure to relatively small quantities of asbestos fibres, they concluded, was directly responsible for the development of cancers, asbestosis and related diseases. Taking into account evidence presented by economists and building industry management, however, the report assumed that, despite the availability of other materials, asbestos would continue to play a major role in the British building industry for many years to come because of its versatility and cost effectiveness.

As a result, the council issued a series of recommendations which were intended to reduce the risks to those who might be exposed to asbestos in working environments. They recommended that, where possible, asbestos-free materials should be employed. In cases where asbestos was employed, it was recommended that it should be used in a bonded form with materials such as cement, so that loose fibres were less likely to enter the air. The report recommended that special care should be taken during work in environments which contain asbestos. Workers should wear protective respiratory equipment and take special care to remove dust from the environment and clothing with the use of vacuum cleaners.

The report isolated five factors which determine the level of risk involved. The state and type of asbestos is critical to determining the risk factor. In addition to the use of bonded forms of asbestos in preference to loose forms, dust formation was found to be limited where the asbestos was worked when wet rather than dry.

The choice of tools was also found to affect the quantities of asbestos particles that enter the air. Machine tools produce greater quantities of dust than hand tools and, where possible, the use of the latter was recommended.

A critical factor in risk reduction is the adequate ventilation of the working environment. Where work takes place in an enclosed space, more asbestos particles circulate and it was therefore recommended that natural or machine ventilation should be used. By rigorously following these guidelines, it was claimed that exposure can be reduced to a reasonably practicable minimum.

The report stated that research carried out by the NMRC showed that the maximum safe level of exposure to blue asbestos was 0.1 fibres per millilitre in an eight-hour working day, whereas as much as 1.0 fibres per millilitre of amosite and chrysotile (white asbestos) could be inhaled. If these levels are strictly adhered to, the report claimed that the onset of asbestosis in a normal working life should not develop.

Critics of the report pointed out that insufficient longitudinal studies had been carried out to determine that the report's recommended maximum safety levels were acceptable.

If, as some as yet unconfirmed data suggest, even minimal exposure to asbestos may result in disease, then clearly the report should have stated that the employment of asbestos was unacceptable in any form.

The claim that 'the onset of asbestosis in a normal working life should not develop if [exposure is maintained within maximum limits]' was cited by critics as evidence of insufficient assurance. Given the time lag which exists between exposure and the diagnosis of asbestos-related diseases, it was unlikely that disease would be diagnosed 'in a normal working lifetime' irrespective of levels of exposure.

Despite these criticisms, the recommended guidelines were incorporated into the working practice of the British Builders' Federation. As a result, it is possible that workers who have been exposed to asbestos may continue to die of asbestos-induced tumours well into the 21st century.

SECTION 2: WRITING

WRITING TASK 1

You should spend no more than 15 minutes on this question.

The dangers of cigarette smoking are now widely recognised. The diagram below illustrates the effects of smoking and outlines possible measures to reduce the risks involved.

> Task: **As a class assignment your tutor has asked you to write about cigarette smoking. Using the diagram below, write three or four paragraphs describing the effects of smoking and methods of risk reduction.**

You may use your own knowledge and experience in addition to the information provided.

Make sure your description is:

- relevant to the question, and
- well organised.

You should write at least 100 words.

> ## SMOKING
>
> EFFECTS: reduced fitness; increased risk of heart disease; lung cancer; respiratory diseases
>
> RECOMMENDED METHODS FOR GIVING UP SMOKING: seek advice from a doctor; consult an acupuncturist; attend smokers' support group
>
> ADVICE FOR SMOKERS: reduce consumption; change to milder brand; use a filter; inhale less smoke

Writing Task 1. Write your answer here.

Writing Task 2

You should spend no more than 30 minutes on this question.

Task: **In almost every country there are laws regulating the content of films, videos, books and newspapers. Should the media be controlled in this way? What are the benefits and risks of censorship?**

You should write a minimum of 250 words.

You should use your own ideas, knowledge and experience and support your arguments with examples and relevant evidence.

NOTES

Writing Task 2. Write your answer here.

IELTS: PRACTICE TESTS

IELTS: PRACTICE TESTS

▶ PRACTICE TEST 3
Academic Module

All answers must be written on the answer sheet.

The test is divided as follows:

- ◢ Reading Passage 1   *Questions 1–10*
- ◢ Reading Passage 2   *Questions 11–16*
- ◢ Reading Passage 3   *Questions 17–23*

Start at the beginning of the test and work through it. You should answer all the questions. If you cannot do a particular question leave it and go on the next one. You can return to it later.

SECTION 1: READING

PART 1: CULTURE AND LEARNING

You are advised to spend about 20 minutes on Questions 1–16.

Questions 1–3

Reading Passage 1: Culture and Learning on pages 31–33 has five sections. From the following list of 12 titles, choose the most suitable title for each of these sections. You can use a title more than once if you wish.

The first one has been done for you as an example.

example: Section I ..F.............................

A. Cultural differences in writing styles
B. Tertiary education
C. Implications for overseas students
D. Academic writing styles
E. International languages

F. Introduction
G. Variation within cultures
H. Subject-specific variations
I. Chemistry and physics
J. Grammatical proficiency

Your answers:

1. Section II   ....
2. Section III   ....
3. Section IV   ....

READING PASSAGE 1: CULTURE AND LEARNING

Section I

Every culture has its own distinctive conventions regarding what should be learned and how learning should take place. These conventions form a largely unquestioned base to the culture's systems of primary, secondary, and tertiary education.

In one culture, students may be encouraged to collaborate with their fellow students, while in another culture this activity may be prohibited. In some societies, students are discouraged from asking questions, while in others they may be required to do so as part of their formal assessment. In some countries, a university lecturer provides students with all the information that they are required to learn; in others, students are required to collect data independently.

A student who undertakes study in a foreign country is faced with a different set of culture-specific conventions. Often these differences are significant enough to require adjustments in learning style and attitudes to knowledge.

Section II

Diversity exists not only between cultures, but also within a single culture. In most British primary and secondary schools, for example, the teacher is the primary provider of required information and rote learning plays an important role in the acquisition of this information. British school leavers who then proceed to university face a new set of academic norms and expectations. Although memorisation is still required, far greater emphasis is placed on the critical evaluation of received information. As they progress through tertiary education, these requirements broaden to include the need to speculate and develop independent research.

Section III

The analysis of writing by students from different cultures suggests that the thinking and writing process is a culture-specific phenomenon. The ability to write well in one language does not necessarily guarantee an equivalent competence in another language, irrespective of an individual's grammatical proficiency in that language.

Although most researchers would agree that writing and thinking are culture-specific phenomena, considerable controversy has been aroused by attempts to provide cognitive profiles for specific cultures. An American study which analysed the way in which students from different cultural backgrounds structured a paragraph of factual writing argued that at least five cognitive profiles could be distinguished.

One profile common to a number of Asian cultures was characterised by an indirect approach to the topic. The paragraph's initial sentences provided background information which led to a concluding sentence in which the main point was described without an explicit judgment.

A second profile was associated with writers of Arabic background. The distinctive feature of this profile was parallelism – ideas were elaborated through repetition and variation.

In contrast to these profiles, the so-called English profile was characterised by a linear movement from a central idea expressed in a summary sentence to an expansion with explanations and examples.

Slavonic and southern European profiles were seen to be similar to the English pattern, differing only in their tolerance of greater diversion from the central point.

Section IV

It may be argued that a similar diversity of cognitive and rhetorical style also exists between academic disciplines. Although standard models for writing reports exist in both chemistry and physics, an adequate physics report may not satisfy the requirements of the chemistry 'sub-culture'.

The departments of tertiary institutions generally publish study guides which provide detailed writing guidelines. These list the rhetorical, referencing and formatting conventions required by each discipline. Before submitting any written work, students are advised to consult appropriate guides and ensure that their written assignments conform to expectations.

Section V

There are, in short, three levels of cultural adjustment which face the overseas undergraduate student: adjustment to a different culturally based learning style; adjustments associated with the move from secondary to tertiary education; and the adjustments related to entry into a specific disciplinary sub-culture.

Questions 4–16
The following passage is a summary of Culture and Learning on pages 31–33. Decide which word or phrase should go in each gap and then write the letter in the space provided. Write only one letter in each space. Note that there are more phrases than gaps. The first one has been done for you as an example.

A. research
B. in one school
C. differing cultural and educational experiences
D. meet
E. the particular academic sub-culture
F. adjust
G. in the same country
H. therefore

I. however
J. knowledge and learning
K. culturally inappropriate
L. a difficulty
M. directly
N. attitudes
O. level of study
P. vary greatly

Summary of 'Culture and Learning'

Because our _example_ to _4_ are conditioned by _5_, students who move to study abroad may need to _6_ their ways of thinking, learning and writing.

_7_ suggests that students from different cultural and linguistic backgrounds are likely to have developed particular ways of writing about arguments and ideas. These different practices may be _8_ if translated _9_ from one culture and language to another. It is not, _10_ possible to generalise about what constitutes the acceptable procedures and practices as these _11_ within a single college or university as a result of factors such as discipline and _12_ This creates _13_ not only for overseas students but also for those who have completed their primary and secondary education ....14.... as that of their tertiary study. Given this situation, students must be aware of the requirements of ....15.... in which they study and be prepared to ....16.... them.

Your answers:

example: ..N..

4.	9.	14 ....
5.	10.	15. ....
6.	11.	16. ....
7.	12.	
8.	13.	

PART 2: FORMAL AND INFORMAL LEARNING

You should spend about 20 minutes on Questions 17–25.

Questions 17–25

By referring to Reading Passage 2: Formal and Informal Learning, decide whether, according to the text, the following statements are true or false by circling A for true or B for false. If the passage does not say, circle C. The first has been done as an example.

	TRUE	FALSE	DOES NOT SAY
example:			
Formal learning is based on conservative methods of teaching.	A	(B)	C
17. Informal learning takes place outside the classroom.	A	B	C
18. Scribner and Cole regard classroom learning as parallel to learning in daily life.	A	B	C
19. Language does not occupy as important a role in informal learning as it does in formal learning.	A	B	C
20. In quoting Bernstein, the author implies that working-class children are disadvantaged by the language used in the classroom.	A	B	C
21. Formal learning excludes the use of sight, touch, taste and smell.	A	B	C
22. Classroom teachers do not provide models of adult behaviour.	A	B	C

	TRUE	FALSE	DOES NOT SAY
23. Adults and older children always seek to provide target models of behaviour for younger children.	A	B	C
24. The informal learner is generally more highly motivated than the formal learner.	A	B	C
25. There may be a link between the absence of holistic education in modern urbanised societies and the incidence of social problems in these societies.	A	B	C

READING PASSAGE 2: FORMAL AND INFORMAL LEARNING

The term 'formal learning' is used in this paper to refer to all learning which takes place in the classroom, irrespective of whether such learning is informed by conservative or progressive ideologies. 'Informal learning', on the other hand, is used to refer to learning which takes place outside the classroom.

These definitions provide the essential, though by no means sole, difference between the two modes of learning. Formal learning is decontextualised from daily life and, indeed, as Scribner and Cole (1973: 553) have observed, may actually 'promote ways of learning and thinking which often run counter to those nurtured in practical daily life'. A characteristic feature of formal learning is the centrality of activities which are not closely paralleled by activities outside the classroom. The classroom can prepare for, draw on, and imitate the challenges of adult life outside the classroom, but it cannot, by its nature, consist of these challenges.

In doing this, language plays a critical role as the major channel for information exchange. 'Success' in the classroom requires a student to master this abstract code. As Bernstein (1969: 152) noted, the language of the classroom is more similar to the language used by middle-class families than that used by working-class families. Middle-class children thus find it easier to acquire the language of the classroom than their working-class peers.

Informal learning, in contrast, occurs in the setting to which it relates, making learning immediately relevant. In this context, language does not occupy such an important role: the child's experience of learning is more holistic, involving sight, touch, taste, and smell—senses that are under-utilised in the classroom.

Whereas formal learning is transmitted by teachers selected to perform this role, informal learning is acquired as a natural part of a child's socialisation. Adults or older children who are proficient in the skill or activity provide—sometimes unintentionally—target models of behaviour in the course of everyday activity. Informal learning, therefore, can take place at any time and is not subject to the limitations imposed by institutional timetabling.

The motivation of the learner provides another critical difference between the two modes of learning. The formal learner is generally motivated by some kind of external goal such as parental approval, social status, and potential financial reward. The informal learner, however, tends to be motivated by successful completion of the task itself and the partial acquisition of adult status.

Given that learning systems develop as a response to the social and economic contexts in which they are embedded, it is understandable that modern, highly urbanised societies have concentrated almost exclusively on the establishment of formal education systems. What these societies have failed to recognise are the ways in which formal learning inhibits the child's multi-sensory acquisition of practical skills. Wolthorpe (1973: 23) speculates that the failure to provide a child with a holistic education may in part account for many of the social problems which plague our societies.

PART 3: APAR ATTITUDES TO KNOWLEDGE AND LEARNING

You should spend about 20 minutes on Questions 26–36.

Questions 26–29

Decide which statements from the list A to G answer questions 26 to 29. Write the letter in the space provided.

A. a series of changes, particularly in the areas of curriculum, teaching methodology, gender segregation, and assessment procedures

B. to identify [Apar] attitudes to and perceptions of knowledge and learning

C. knowledge of the skills required to perform domestic and agricultural tasks is not endowed with spiritual significance and has indeed evolved with changes in technology

D. it was hypothesised that these attitudes and perceptions would correspond to other sociocultural indicators and would in part account for low academic performance and completion rates

E. attitudes and perceptions were elicited by means of a semi-structured interview

F. the data exhibited a high degree of similarity between children, parents, and teachers

G. the centralised curriculum implemented in Apar schools was at variance with these world views and learning styles

Your answers:

26. Aim of research ....

27. Research methodology ....

28. Conclusion ....

29. Recommendations ....

READING PASSAGE 3: APAR ATTITUDES TO KNOWLEDGE AND LEARNING

The low school-completion rates and below-average academic performance of non-urban minorities have attracted the attention of educational researchers specialising in culture-specific attitudes to knowledge and learning. Obudu and Banga (1967) focused on this phenomenon among the Apar, a hill-tribe which until the 1950s had no experience of classroom-based education.

Obudu and Banga interviewed 110 children aged between 10 and 12, their parents, and 50 teachers working in Apar schools. The aim of the project was to identify their attitudes to and perceptions of knowledge and learning. It was hypothesised that these attitudes and perceptions would correspond to other sociocultural indicators and would in part account for low academic performance and completion rates. Attitudes and perceptions were elicited by means of a semi-structured interview. Data from these interviews were then encoded using the Egloff-Waas system.

The data exhibited a high degree of similarity between children, parents, and teachers. Obudu and Banga (1968: 96) summarised their findings as follows. The Apar distinguish two types of knowledge. Spiritual knowledge is regarded as a divine gift, which constitutes a source of power, and hence is transmitted from tribal elders to young male initiates in ritualised ceremonies. This knowledge is, moreover, unchanging and cannot be challenged. In contrast, knowledge of the skills required to perform domestic and agricultural tasks is not endowed with spiritual significance and has indeed evolved with changes in technology. A further characteristic of this kind of knowledge is the demarcation of knowledge areas according to gender.

Preferences in learning style among the Apar relate to these views of knowledge. The study identified a marked preference for two styles of learning: the passive and respectful acceptance of knowledge from a revered male figure, and observation and imitation of adults in their performance of tasks perceived as relevant to the respective genders of the children.

Obudu and Banga argued that the centralised curriculum implemented in Apar schools was at variance with these world views and learning styles. The importance given to linguistically complex problem-based learning, for example, was perceived as irrelevant by the majority of the subjects. Similarly, examinations which required students to write essays expressing their personal opinions were not only perceived as irrelevant, but also profoundly offensive.

Based on these findings, Obudu and Banga recommended a series of changes in the areas of curriculum, teaching methodology, gender segregation, and assessment procedures. In a pilot project carried out in 1974, these changes were made in the newly established Bititi Experimental High School in the Apar region.

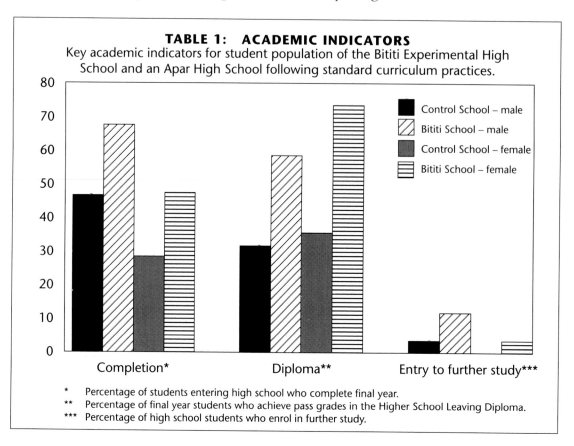

TABLE 1: ACADEMIC INDICATORS
Key academic indicators for student population of the Bititi Experimental High School and an Apar High School following standard curriculum practices.

Legend:
- Control School – male
- Bititi School – male
- Control School – female
- Bititi School – female

Categories: Completion*, Diploma**, Entry to further study***

* Percentage of students entering high school who complete final year.
** Percentage of final year students who achieve pass grades in the Higher School Leaving Diploma.
*** Percentage of high school students who enrol in further study.

Questions 30–36

Decide whether Table 1 supports, rejects, or does not discuss the following statements.

Circle the appropriate letter: A, B, or C.

	SUPPORTED	REJECTED	NO EVIDENCE
30. In both schools, completion rates among females are lower than those of males.	A	B	C
31. In both schools, proportionately fewer males than females achieve pass grades in the Diploma exam.	A	B	C
32. Fewer females than males enrol in high school.	A	B	C
33. The majority of students at both schools do not go on to further study.	A	B	C

	SUPPORTED	REJECTED	NO EVIDENCE
34. The percentage of control school males who complete high school is higher than the percentage of Bititi females who complete high school.	A	B	C
35. Table 1 provides data which suggest that the Obudu and Banga recommendations were appropriate to Apar learners.	A	B	C
36. Bititi students are more diligent than their control school counterparts.	A	B	C

SECTION 2: WRITING

WRITING TASK 1

You should spend no more than 15 minutes on this task.

You have been asked to write a report for a scholarship committee on the adjustments that overseas students need to make.

> Task: **Describe the most important adjustments to learning and writing styles you feel overseas students are likely to need to make and give advice on how they should do this.**

You should write a minimum of 250 words.

You should use your own ideas, knowledge and experience and support your arguments with examples and relevant evidence.

Writing Task 1. Write your answer here.

IELTS: PRACTICE TESTS

WRITING TASK 2

You should spend no more than 40 minutes on this task.

> Task: It is often said that the subjects taught in schools are too academic in orientation and that it would be more useful for children to learn about practical matters such as home management, work and interpersonal skills. To what extent do you agree? Which subjects should be taught in school in your opinion? Write an essay for a university lecturer making appropriate recommendations.

You should write a minimum of 250 words.

You should use your own ideas, knowledge and experience and support your arguments with examples and relevant evidence.

NOTES

Writing Task 2. Write your answer here.

IELTS: PRACTICE TESTS

► PRACTICE TEST 4
General Training Module

SECTION 1: READING

PART 1

You should spend 15 minutes on Questions 1–12.

Questions 1–2

Read the following newspaper advertisements and answer the questions below each one. Choose which of the alternatives A, B, C or D is the correct answer and write that letter in the space provided. The first one has been done as an example.

> NEAR BEACH. Mod 2 b.r. unfurnished flat on third floor overlooking beach. Close shops/bus. $195 p.w. Tel 45 6345 before 11 a.m.

This advertisement is for

A. a house

B. furniture

C. a school

D. an apartment

Your answer: ....D...........................

1.

> Casual kitchen hand required for busy hotel restaurant. Mornings only. Friendly atmosphere. No experience necessary. Tel 799 9560.

This advertisement is for

A. a hotel

B. a job

C. a training course

D. a new kitchen

Your answer: ....

2.

> COMMUNICATION SKILLS. Do you want to improve the way you communicate and relate to other people? Mondays 7–9 p.m. for six weeks. Cost: $75

This advertisement is for

A. a book

B. a video cassette

C. a film

D. a course

Your answer: ....

Questions 3-5

Read the information on the following drivers licence and answer the questions. The first one has been done as an example.

DRIVER'S LICENCE

Liliana Aranda   Licence expires
8 Young St   07 JULY 1998
Newtown 3474   **Licence No: 3011FA**

Change of address must be notified within 7 days by telephoning 566 4000.

THIS LICENCE MAY BE CANCELLED FOR FAILURE
TO COMPLY STRICTLY WITH THE TRAFFIC LAWS.

Unless previously suspended or cancelled, this licence must be renewed on or before the date of expiry.

If this card is found please hand it in at any Motor Registry.

---

example:

When will the licence expire?

07 July 1998

3. What must Liliana do if she changes her address?

   _____

   _____

   _____

4. What might happen if Liliana does not obey the traffic laws?

   _____

   _____

   _____

5. If you find Liliana's licence, what should you do?

   _____

   _____

   _____

Questions 6-8

Read the following notice in a residential college and then answer the questions following.

MORETON COLLEGE, DURHAM, ENGLAND
Welcome to Moreton College!
After you settle in, we would like to orient you to the facilities (and regulations!) of our College. Orientation sessions will be held as follows. Please ensure that you attend on time.

First-year students:	6.00 p.m. in the Bay Room
Second-year students:	7.00 p.m. in the Reid Room

Please note that there is a special orientation session for foreign students. All foreign students (whether first-year or second-year) should go to the Reid Room at 8.30 p.m.

Your answers:

6. You are a foreign first-year student.
   Which room should you go to?   ....

7. You are an English second-year student.
   What time is your orientation session?   ....

8. You are a foreign second-year student.
   What time is your orientation session?   ....

Questions 9–12

Below there is a page from the local telephone directory giving information about various services. Read the following situations and decide which number you should telephone.

Write the numbers in the space provided. The first one has been done as an example.

INSTANT CALL GUIDE

Directory Assistance
For unknown, new and altered numbers
Local 019
International 055

Faults and Service Difficulties
Local 088
International 044
Business Customer Faults 008

Operator Connected Calls
From a private phone............................. 076
From a payphone.................................... 042
Charge enquiries.................................... 066
International Telegrams............................. 093
Wake up/reminder calls 012
Telephone bill enquiries............................17489

---

example:

You want to send an international telegram

Your answer: ...*093*..............................

9. You are trying to call locally but the telephone is not working properly ....

10. You want to know how much it will cost to telephone your home country. ....

11. You have to telephone your local kindergarten but you do not know the number. ....

12. Your international phone call was cut off while you were speaking. ....

PART 2

You are advised to spend 20 minutes on Questions 13–25.

Questions 13–18

Don't Pay Full Fare on page 49 is an article from a local newspaper. Decide whether, according to the article the following sentences are correct. Circle A if a sentence is correct, B if it is incorrect, and C if the information is not given. The first one has been done as an example.

	CORRECT	INCORRECT	NO INFORMATION GIVEN
example:			
You can buy a standby ticket the day before you travel.	A	(B)	C
13. University students must be under 26 years of age in order to qualify for a student discount.	A	B	C
14. The Common Interest Group scheme does not apply if there are 11 adults in the group.	A	B	C
15. Only students can qualify for the standby discount	A	B	C
16. Secondary students can travel only during secondary school vacations.	A	B	C
17. Most secondary students are aged between 15 and 19.	A	B	C
18. There is no 'stay away' minimum for secondary students.	A	B	C

DON'T PAY FULL FARE

Are you taking advantage of the discounts available on airfares? If not, then you are unnecessarily paying too much.

Most airlines now have a number of options which can give the traveller up to 50 per cent discount on the full economy fare on both domestic and international flights.

Students benefit most from the discount systems, with two schemes available. Students between the ages of 15 and 19 who are registered in full-time day courses at secondary institutions can receive 50 per cent discount, while full-time students attending a recognised university or college receive a 25 per cent discount, provided that they are under 26 years of age. In both cases, the air tickets are valid for one year and there is no minimum 'stay away' period. Although not required, students travelling on these tickets are advised to pay early in order to insure against subsequent price increases.

If you are not a student, do not despair. You may qualify for the Common Interest Group system, if you are one of at least ten adults who are 'travelling together for a common purpose on one flight between the same origin/destination'. If you qualify, you will receive a 15 per cent discount on your ticket. Again, the tickets are valid for one year and there is no minimum 'stay away' period. Full payment for the tickets must be made at least 48 hours prior to departure.

Finally, if you can accept the uncertainty, you might consider the so-called 'standby' system. In this scheme, which gives a 20 per cent discount, you purchase your ticket at the airport on the day of travel, assuming of course that there are empty seats on the flight of your choice. With standby tickets there is no minimum and no maximum 'stay away' period.

These are just some of the schemes available to air travellers. Before parting with your hard-earned cash, do check with your local travel agent about your eligibility for the various discounts available. Just remember: 'Don't pay the full fare!'

Questions 19–25

Read the information about casual employment in the hospitality industry given below and answer the following questions. Where you are given a choice of four possible answers (for example Question 22), put A, B, C or D in the spaces provided

19. What is the minimum period of casual engagement on a public holiday?

20. At what time in the evening do overtime penalty rates begin?

21. Who is responsible for providing clothing such as waistcoats?

22. Casual employees must be given a free meal or a meal allowance if they:

    A. work after 7.00 a.m.   C. work over five hours a day

    B. have had 12 months' service   D. are paid $5.00

23. On 1 May 1996 meal allowances and laundry allowances will:

    A. be increased   C. decrease

    B. be terminated   D. be paid at the overtime rate

24. In casual employment, notice of termination is:
    A. not possible   C. provided
    B. not necessary   D. paid in lieu

25. Which of the following sentences best sums up the situation of casual staff?
    A. The employers of casual staff are   C. Casual staff must provide their
       well protected by regulations.   own uniforms.
    B. The rights and conditions of   D. The conditions of casual staff are
       casual staff are clearly specified.   as good as those of full-time staff.

Your answers:

19. ....

20. ....

21. ....

22. ....

23. ....

24. ....

25. ....

CASUAL EMPLOYMENT

A casual employee is one who is engaged and paid as such by agreement between the employer and employee. There is a three-hour minimum payment for each period of engagement and a four-hour minimum engagement on a Public Holiday. No notice of termination of is required. For night work between 8.00 p.m. and 7.00 a.m. Monday to Friday a penalty of $1.28 per hour (or part of hour) shall be paid with a minimum of $4.37 for any one day on which such hours are worked.

Meals: Casual employees whose engagement extends for five hours or more shall be provided with a meal free of charge, or shall be paid in lieu of $5.00 ($6.00 from 1 May l996).

Casual employment over eight hours: Paid at the overtime rate of full time employees.

Payment of wages: By mutual consent either weekly or on termination of engagement.

Annual leave: Pro-rata Annual Leave entitlement for casuals is on the basis of 1/12th of earnings. Many employers pay this inclusive with the hourly rate. If this is not done, it should be paid on termination of services or at the end of 12 months' service.

Special clothing: A casual employee is required to provide and wear a black and white uniform or an equivalent standard specified by the club (e.g. blue and white, cook's clothing, etc.) This includes bow tie and cummerbund if required. Any other special clothing such as fancy coats, waistcoats, etc. must be provided by the employer. The employer may launder all uniforms, or pay the employee an allowance of $1.00 per engagement ($1.20 from 1 May 1996) for general staff. Cooks shall be paid $1.50 per engagement ($1.70 from 1 May 1996).

PART 3

You are advised to spend 25 minutes on Questions 26–40.

Questions 26–31

Read the passage below, then fill in each gap with ONE word from the box below the passage. You may use a word more than once if you wish. Write your answers in the spaces following the passage. The first one has been done as an example.

Use Electricity Safely

Most electrical accidents in the home *example* because people fail to observe basic safety procedures. Always switch off at the powerpoint before you remove the plug. Always remove the plug by grasping it—not by ...26... the cord. Check to see that the power is ...27... off when changing lightbulbs. Do not use electrical appliances ...28... a swimming pool. A shock could cause paralysis, resulting in drowning. Check the ...29... of leads and extension cords regularly to ensure that they are functioning properly Switch off appliances if the power ...30.... Fires have been caused when power returns unexpectedly. Teach children that electrical appliances, cords and switches are not toys. Insert safety plugs in powerpoints to ...31... young children.

Your answers:

example: *occur*

26. ....

27. ....

28. ....

29. ....

30. ....

31. ....

avoid	accident	warning
condition	near	switched
removed	protect	touch
fails	pulling	
occur	tested	

Questions 32–40

Read the Useful Hints for using a gas cooker on page 53, and answer the following questions.

32. If you want to cook food rapidly, which burner should you use?

33. If the flame is too high,
       A. gas is wasted   C. the worktop is scorched
       B. the pan is placed centrally   D. it produces deposits

34. A 'moderate' oven is ... a 'warm' oven.
       A. not as hot as   C. hotter than
       B. the equivalent of   D. at the same time as

35. How long does it take the oven to become 'very hot'?

36. When grilling food, the grill door
       A. must be kept open   C. must not overhang the side
       B. must be set to 'MAX'   D. must be removed

37. Various dishes ... be cooked at the same time in the oven.
       A. must   C. cannot
       B. can   D. need to

38. What kind of utensils should not be kept in the storage drawer?

39. Which system of temperature is used on the oven control knob?

40. Cooking utensils may be made of a range of materials, but they must be
       A. flammable   C. steady
       B. preheated   D. ceramic

Your answers:

32. ....

33. ....

34. ....

35. ....

36. ....

37. ....

38. ....

39. ....

40. ....

USING YOUR *SCORPIO* COOKER: USEFUL HINTS

Follow these useful hints to obtain the best results when using your new SCORPIO cooker.

Choice of burner

Use large burner to bring liquids to the boil quickly, brown meat and generally for all food that is cooked rapidly. Use small burners for stewed dishes and sauces.

To conserve gas, place the pan centrally over the burner and adjust the flame so that it does not extend past the edges of the pan.

Do not boil food too rapidly. A strong boil does not cook any faster but violently shakes up the food, which may then lose its taste.

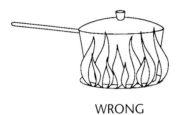

WRONG
flame too high – wastes gas

CORRECT
flame not past edges of pan – conserves gas

Utensils

All normally available utensils (aluminium, stainless steel, cast iron, ceramic, etc.) may be used on your new gas cooker, but ensure that they are steady, in order to avoid dangerous spill-over of hot liquids.

> *Caution: Large Utensils*
> When a cooker is installed close to a worktop, ensure that whenever large utensils are used, they are placed so that they do not overhang the side of the hotplate, as this may cause scorching or charring of the worktop surface.

> *Warning: Asbestos Mats*
> Do not use asbestos mats as they tend to cause a temperature build-up which can damage the enamel.

Griller

The grill burner has variable settings, the high setting being denoted by 'MAX' and the low setting by 'MIN' on the griller control knob.

> *Note: The grill door should be left open during grilling.*

Oven

When using recipes that refer to temperatures in degrees Fahrenheit, the conversion scale located on the splashback will provide a ready means of finding the equivalent in degrees Celsius so that the oven control knob can readily be set to the correct temperature. This is the temperature on the second shelf from the bottom. There is a gradual variation in temperature between the bottom and top of the oven. The first, or bottom, shelf position is the coolest and the fourth, or top, shelf position is the hottest. Because of the temperature variation from one shelf position to another, it is possible to cook various dishes which require different temperatures, at the same time. As a rough guide, the temperature variation from one shelf to the next is about ten degrees Celsius.

Some recipes do not refer directly to temperature but use descriptions such as 'slow', 'moderate', 'hot', etc. When using such recipes, the following chart may be taken as a guide:

OVEN TEMPERATURES		
slow	:	110°C
warm	:	130°C
moderate	:	150°C
moderately hot	:	180°C
hot	:	220°C
very hot	:	250°C

If preheating is required, allow time for the oven to reach the set temperature. The following table may be used as a guide:

PREHEATING		
3 minutes	:	120°C
6 minutes	:	180°C
10 minutes	:	250°C

Note that the oven light (where fitted) is located on the splashback.

> *Caution: Polyunsaturated Oil*
> Do not use polyunsaturated oil in oven cooking as it can cause heavy plastic film-type deposits on the inside of the oven which can be very difficult to remove from normal enamel and glass.

Storage drawer (where fitted)
The storage drawer situated underneath the oven is designed for the storage of pans and utensils. Do not place plastic utensils or flammable material in this drawer. To remove the drawer, withdraw it to the fully open position. Then lift it clear of the stops. To refit the drawer, locate the nylon drawer slides on the slide tracks. Lift the drawer slightly to clear the stops, then slide it to the fully shut position.

SECTION 2: WRITING

WRITING TASK 1

You should spend no more than 20 minutes on this task.

You have been accepted at Moreton College, a residential college at your new university. You are expected to arrive on 25 February to attend the college orientation session, but you will not be able to arrive by that date.

> TASK: Write to the Principal of the College explaining why you will be delayed, expressing your concern about missing the orientation session, and asking what you should do.

You should write at least 150 words.

You do **NOT** need to write your address.

The Principal,
Moreton College
University of Durham
Durham City
England DH2 4KY

_____

_____

_____

_____

_____

_____

_____

_____

_____

_____

_____

_____

_____

_____

_____

_____

_____

_____

_____

_____

_____

_____

WRITING TASK 2

You should spend no more than 40 minutes on this task.

As part of getting to know the other students in your residential college, you have been asked to write a statement about yourself.

> TASK: Give a BRIEF description of your study plans. THEN write a short account of your reasons for deciding to study in this particular English-speaking country.

You should write at least 250 words.

NOTES

Writing Task 2. Write your answer here.

_____
_____
_____
_____
_____
_____
_____
_____
_____
_____
_____
_____
_____
_____
_____
_____
_____
_____
_____
_____
_____
_____
_____

▶ PRACTICE LISTENING TEST

Time allowed: *30 minutes*

In order to take this test, you should listen to side B of the accompanying cassette. Remember that you must answer the questions as you listen.

SECTION 1

Questions 1–4

Which of the pictures best fits what you hear on the tape? Circle the letter under that picture. The first one has been done for you as an example.

example:

Which room does the woman want?

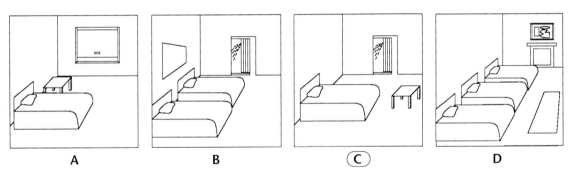

A   B   C   D

1. Which is the Evandale Hotel?

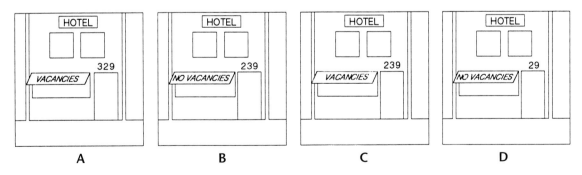

A   B   C   D

2. What time does Mark arrive at the hotel?

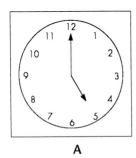

A

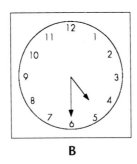

B

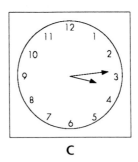

C

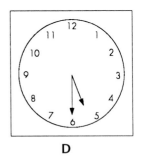

D

3. Which room does Mark stay in?

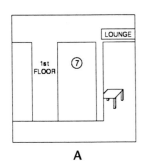

A

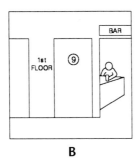

B

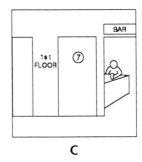

C

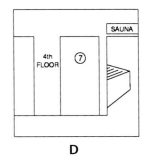

D

4. Who is Mark waiting for?

A

B

C

D

Questions 5–9

Fill in the numbered gaps.

Evandale Hotel Registration Form

5. Surname: ....

　First name: *Mark* ....

6. Home address: *42 North Road,* ....

7. Postcode: .... *Cheshire* ....

8. Nationality: ....

9. Arrival date: *August 9* ....

　Departure date: ....

Questions 10 and 11

10. How does Mark travel from the hotel to the city centre?

 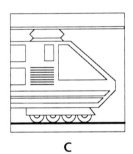 

A   B   C   D

11. Where is the Consulate located?

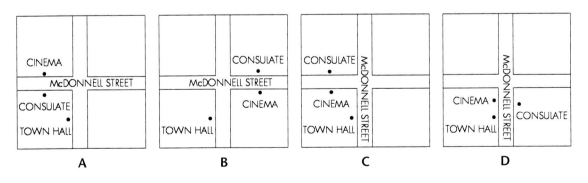

SECTION 2

Fill in the gaps in this news report by writing the missing words in the column on the right.

Questions 12–19

Inter-city express ___12___ bound for ___13___ has crashed near Rugby about an hour after leaving London. The train crashed into a stationary goods train which was on the main line. At least ___14___ people have been killed including the train's ___15___ . The ___16___ part of the train has been destroyed. Rescuers are trying to free passengers from two of the carriages which are lying on their ___17___ . Investigators believe a failure of ___18___ may be responsible for the accident. Anyone wanting information about the incident should ring ___19___ .

Your answers:

12. ....

13. ....

14. ....

15. ....

16. ....

17. ....

18. ....

19. ....

SECTION 3

Questions 20–28

Decide whether the following statements are true or false according to the passage. Circle T for 'True' or F for 'False'. The first one has been done as an example.

example:

The conversation class is held twice a week.	T	(F)
20. A writing skills course IS offered in the first six weeks of semester.	T	F
21. The writing skills course is designed for students in the departments of Biological Science and Economics.	T	F
22. The examination skills class only prepares students for written examinations.	T	F
23. Only postgraduates can attend the research report writing course.	T	F
24. Students do not need to obtain an enrolment form for the research report writing course.	T	F
25. Individual consultations are not available during the vacation.	T	F
26. The Independent Learning Centre is closed on Friday afternoons.	T	F
27. Students need a special borrowing card to borrow books from the Independent Learning Centre.	T	F
28. Students must pay for Language classes.	T	F

SECTION 4

Questions 29–38

Answer questions 29 to 38 by writing a word or a short phrase in the space provided. The first one is done for you as an example.

example:

How long has she been working for the Canadian export agency?

three years

29. Which two countries does she specialise in?

30. What did she find most difficult when she started the job?

31. What kind of products were exhibited at the Beijing fair?

32. How long does it usually take her to plan a trade fair?

33. What does she do while flying?

34. Where does she usually meet government officials?

35. What did her parents want her to study?

36. What does she need legal knowledge for?

37. What foreign languages does she speak?

38. Why is she excited about the fashion fair in Tokyo?

Section 1

Speaker: Mr and Mrs Nelson, the owners of a private hotel, are waiting for a guest to check in. Study the example and questions 1 to 4. For each question there are four pictures. Decide which of the pictures best corresponds to what you hear on the tape. Circle the letter under that picture. The first one has been done for you as an example.

Answer the questions while you listen as the tape is only played once.

Mrs Nelson: Hello, Evandale Hotel. Can I help you?

Enquirer: Yes, Good afternoon. I wonder if you have a single room with a private bathroom for tonight, please?

Mrs Nelson: Let me just check ... single room with private bathroom just for tonight. Yes we have a vacancy. Would you like to make a booking?

Enquirer: No. I'll come around now if that's OK. What's the address please?

Mrs Nelson: 239 Marsh Street.

Enquirer: I'll just write that down—239 Marsh Street. OK I'll see you in about twenty minutes.

Mrs Nelson: Goodbye. Cyril, we've got a guest coming. We can put her in number 8.

....

Mr Nelson: Dear me, it's getting dark earlier and earlier. What time is it, Mavis?

Mrs Nelson: 4.30.

Mr Nelson: Oh ... that Mr Crystal should be checking in soon, shouldn't he?

Mrs Nelson: He said in his letter that his flight was due in at 3.15 and that he'd be coming straight here from the airport. By the time he gets here it'll probably be 5 o'clock. There's a lot of traffic at this time of day. Wait a minute—there's someone coming in now.

Mr Nelson: Hello, good to see you, you must be Mr Crystal. How was your flight?

Mr Crystal: Not too bad. Once I've had a shower and a shave, though, I'll be a different person .

Mrs Nelson: Hello Mr Crystal. You got in earlier than we expected. It's just gone half past four.

Mr Crystal: Yes, well the traffic wasn't too bad. My flight came in ten minutes early as well . . .

Mr Nelson: ... and that's the TV lounge over there. Now, breakfast is at 8 and dinner at 6.30. Well, here's the key to your room. I think you'll like it. Number seven's on the first floor next door to the bar. It's got a lovely view. It looks onto the river and the park.

Mr Crystal: Oh by the way, I m expecting somebody over in about half an hour. As soon as I've unpacked I'll come downstairs so could you tell him that I'll be waiting in the TV lounge?

Mrs Nelson: Yes certainly.

Mr Crystal: He's an American—a very tall man with glasses—you can't miss him.

Mr Nelson: I'll keep an eye open for him. Oh by the way, will you be wanting an early morning alarm call?

Speaker: Mr Nelson then asks Mr Crystal to fill in a registration form. As you listen to the tape fill in the gaps numbered five to nine on the form. Now look at the registration form. Now listen and fill in the gaps numbered 5 to 9.

Mr Nelson: Now one final thing—I'll just have to fill in the registration form, Mr Crystal and then I'll take your things up to your room. So it's Mr Crystal—that's C-R-Y-S-T-A-L, is that right?

Mr Crystal: That's right, Mark Crystal.

Mr Nelson: Mark ... and your home address, Mr Crystal?

Mr Crystal: 42 North Road, Cheadle—that's C-H-E-A-D-L-E—in Cheshire.

Mr Nelson: And the postcode please?

Mr Crystal: Oh ... Let's see if I remember, S-K-8 ... 4 R-T

Mr Nelson: OK and you're a British citizen?

Mr Crystal: Yes.

Mr Nelson: Right you are, sir. You'll be staying here from tonight until Thursday morning? OK. Today's the ninth so that'll be August the twelfth. If you'd like to come this way I'll take your bags up for you.

Speaker: Later that afternoon, after his meeting, Mr Crystal asks Mrs Nelson for street directions. As you listen decide which picture best fits the information given. First look at questions 10 and 11.

Mrs Nelson: Hello Mr Crystal. Your visitor found you?

Mr Crystal: Yes thanks. Listen, listen, I have to get into town. Which is the best way to get to the city centre from here?

Mrs Nelson: It's not very far at all. There's a taxi-rank in the square just at the end of the street here or you could even walk. It's about half an hour's walk if you're not feeling too jet-lagged! There's a train service from Miller Street Station but it'd take you about ten minutes to get to the station from here. What part of the city do you want?

Mr Crystal: I need to get to the American Consulate. Do you know where that is?

Mrs Nelson: Let me have a look. Oh right. Your best bet in that case would be the bus. There's a stop on the opposite side of this road. Can you see it? Just past that red coach. You can get a 45 and get off at the Town Hall. It's ... let me see one, two, three yeah three stops down. Better ask the conductor to tell you when you're there just to be on the safe side. When you're at Town Hall just keep on walking to the end of the block, turn left into McDonnell Street and you'll see a big cinema on the right. The consulate's just opposite. You can't miss it.

Mr Crystal: Yeah, yeah. Opposite the cinema in McDonnell Street. That sounds easy enough. Thanks very much. See you at dinner. Six o'clock wasn't it?

Speaker: That is the end of the first section. You now have thirty seconds to check your answers.

Speaker: Now turn to Section 2.

Mark listens to a radio news bulletin in his hotel bedroom. You should fill in the gaps numbered 12 to 19 in the summary of the news item by writing the missing words in the column on the right of the passage. First read questions 12 to 19.

Now listen to the news bulletin and answer questions 12 to 19.

Radio Newsreader: A serious rail crash occurred in the early hours of this morning near Rugby, about one hundred and fifty kilometres north-west of London. The Inter-city express No. 895 from London Euston bound for Liverpool collided with a stationary goods train about five kilometres from Rugby station. Seven people have been killed including the driver of the express. Thirty other passengers have been hurt. The injured have been taken to Rugby Hospital where some are in a critical condition. Rescue operations are still in progress and the fire brigade is attempting to free some passengers and railway staff who are still trapped in the wreckage. Our reporter Nora Martingale- Stuart is at the scene. What's the situation, Nora?

Nora Martingale-Stuart: Pretty bad I'm afraid, Pat. A scene of total destruction but the rescue services got here very quickly—about ten minutes after the crash—so they've been working for about an hour now in very difficult conditions. It's still dark here of course and the police, fire brigade and medical teams are using arc lights to work by. The front part of the train—the locomotive and first two carriages—are still on the tracks but they've been completely destroyed and there's no hope for anyone who was in them, I'm afraid. The rescue teams are working to free people who are trapped inside the two rear carriages which have been derailed, and are lying on their sides at the bottom of an embankment. I've got with me Chief Officer Briggs of the Rugby Fire Brigade who's co-ordinating the Emergency Services here. Mr Briggs, how long do you reckon it'll be before you can get any remaining survivors out?

Chief Officer Briggs: It's hard to say. The front two carriages have really been concertinaed and there's not much hope for anyone who was in there. We just don't know how many were travelling in that section but as it's a holiday weekend it was probably fairly full. There are at least five passengers trapped beneath the wreckage of the third carriage and we know that at least two of them are still alive. The carriage is lying on its side and the fire services are using oxy-acetylene cutting equipment to get through. We should have them out quite soon.

Nora Martingale-Stuart: Thank you, Officer Briggs. A team of crash investigators is already trying to understand why the goods train was on the main line. One theory concerns a new signalling light which came into operation on this section of the line only last week. It's believed that a failure of the light may be responsible but investigators are not at present ruling out other possibilities. If there are any other details we'll let you know as soon as we have them. In the meantime it's back to you in the studio, Pat.

Newsreader: Thank you, Nora. We'll bring you more news as it comes in. An emergency hotline has been set up by the Rugby police. Those requiring information are requested to ring the following toll-free number 008 76935. I'll repeat that again, 008 76935. And now for international news. In Sierra Leone ...

Speaker: That is the end of the second section. You now have thirty seconds to check your answers.

Speaker: Section 3. Sayeed attends an introductory talk given by the Co-ordinator of the English for Academic Purposes department in his college. As you listen to the recording answer questions 20 to 28 by circling T for 'True' and F for 'False'. The first question has been done for you as an example. First you should read questions 20 to 28.

Now answer questions 20 to 28.

Rohan Davidson: Morning, everyone and welcome to the English for Academic Purposes Centre. I m Rohan Davidson, the co-ordinator here, and I'd like to begin by giving you a brief run-down of the services which we offer here at our centre. First of all, we have a wide range of language classes. In first semester we run a conversation class for students of non-English-speaking backgrounds who wish to improve their fluency, grammar and pronunciation in English. This is held in Room W5A 209—that's on level two of the Branson Block—on Tuesdays between 12.30 and 1.30. So that's one hour once a week. The teacher is Ms Marion Elsdon. If you'd like to participate in this class, please enrol with the secretary on level six of Building C5A before Friday, July 23rd.

For those of you interested in developing your writing skills we have a six-week course which runs for two hours between 4 and 6 on Wednesday afternoons beginning in week one. It concentrates on the writing skills needed for assignments in the Departments of Economics and Social Sciences. Students must be enrolled in either of these departments.

You're probably not thinking about taking examinations yet but later on towards the end of term you might like to enrol in our Examination Skills class run by Mr Ted Schegloff in the School of English and Linguistics. The course runs for five weeks and deals with the skills you need in both written tests and those examinations where you are interviewed and therefore have to speak. It is not necessary to enrol before the course starts. Just turn up for the first class.

A new course that we're running this year is a research report writing course, beginning on August 25th. The course is designed for postgraduate students in any discipline. If you're interested in this course but you're doing an undergraduate course you're still welcome to attend. You must, however, get an enrolment form before beginning the course so please ring Ms Melanie Woo on extension 6744 or come to the Postgraduate Students Office.

Some of you may feel the need for more individual attention, especially when you've got assignments to write. The language advisers are available for consultations and you can book an appointment by ringing 666 0933 between 9.30 and midday, Monday to Friday. Remember that the service doesn't operate during vacation—only in term-time and please try to book an appointment as early as possible. Don't leave it all until the last day just before you've got an assignment to hand in.

We hope you'll take advantage of the Independent Learning Centre on the fourth floor of the Springvale Building. The centre offers grammar books, audio and video-cassettes, word-processing facilities and other study skills aids to all students at the university The centre is open between 4 and 6 Monday to Thursday and until midday on Fridays. You can borrow all books and tapes except master copies and reference works for up to a week but you must get an ILC borrowing card. To do this it's very simple—just come along to the front desk with an ID card and we'll do it straight away. You can borrow up to three books or tapes at a time but these are only available for borrowing between Thursdays and Tuesdays. Marie and Louise, who are the Centre Supervisors, are on hand to answer any questions you may have and help you find the materials you need.

I should add, by the way, that you don't have to pay for any of our classes or other services. Providing you're enrolled in full or part-time courses at the university, they're all free of charge. We do make a charge of thirty pence a copy for any photocopying made at the centre. That's all. Well, I look forward to seeing you here during the year and remember if you've got any problems don't hesitate to contact me here.

Speaker: That is the end of the third section. You now have thirty seconds to check your answers.

Speaker: Section 4. Chris, who works for the Canadian Export Development Agency, is being interviewed on a radio program called 'My Career'. Listen to the interview and answer questions 29 to 38 by writing a word or a short phrase in the space provided. The first one is done for you as an example. Now look at questions 29 to 38.

Now answer questions 29 to 38.

Interviewer: Tonight we have Chris Davenport with us in the studio. Welcome to the program, Chris.

Chris: Thank you, Pat.

Interviewer: Now, Chris, you've been working for the Canadian Export Agency for three years now.

Chris: Yes, that's right.

Interviewer: And what does your job involve?

Chris: Well, my particular brief is the Asian section – especially Japan and China. Now, we work with Canadian firms explaining how they can start up or develop their export trade in these countries. One of my main responsibilities is to set up trade fairs so that our companies can exhibit their goods in these other countries. We'd organise between two and three trade fairs in these regions each year so, as you can see, I do a lot of organising and a lot of travelling.

Interviewer: Right. Sounds like a very demanding job. How do you cope with the pressures?

Chris: Well, at first I didn't. It was very difficult because there were so many new things to learn and I found especially that negotiating was the hardest. It was something that didn't come to me naturally, but you get used to it.

Interviewer: What's the secret?

Chris: Well, you have to be organised, especially well organised, but it does help of course that we're part of a team and when the going gets rough we give each other a lot of support and help each other out. That's important. I've just recently come back from Beijing where we sponsored an electronics fair there. We had a total of fifty-five stands and we had over two hundred thousand visitors.

Interviewer: Two hundred! Wow!

Chris: Two hundred thousand. Yeh. It was very successful but it did represent twelve months of really intensive preparation and, as you can guess, a lot of difficult negotiations.

Interviewer: Twelve months?! I mean, is that normal, Chris?

Chris: Well, it does vary a lot. Beijing – twelve months – was a particularly large trade fair and it did take that kind of time. But some of our smaller fairs, Canton for example, we had a small computing exhibition there in '89. That took five months of planning. As a general rule, it takes about six months. That's not a hard and fast rule, but basically about six months, depending on the kind of product being exhibited, the network of contacts we already have in the host country, the location, things like that.

Interviewer: Right. Sounds like an exciting job.

Chris: Yes. People say "Oh, all that lovely travel abroad". And travel abroad's terrific in a holiday, but this is not holiday—it's work. When you spend twenty hours on a plane maybe six, seven times a year, it becomes very tiring, because you don't go off sightseeing after—you go to work. I also work on the plane of course, catching up on paperwork, writing reports on the laptop, things like that. Then when we arrive at the destination, it's straight from the airport to our office for a series of planning meetings. My first responsibility is to meet with the government officials in the host country. We used to meet in our offices in the embassy or in their departmental offices but we found it much more comfortable for everyone to meet in informal settings like restaurants. People just seem to be more relaxed and its better for negotiations. Amongst my other tasks, I arrange accommodation for exhibitors, I organise for interpreters, and I help out on the legal side. So I guess that makes me partly international lawyer and partly tour guide. It's hard work but rewarding.

Interviewer: Right. So, you mentioned law. Did you study law at college?

Chris: Yes, I did. Yes. I have a Bachelor's Degree in Legal Studies.

Interviewer: OK. And have you ever practised as a lawyer?

Chris: No. No, I haven't actually. Before I went to college I really wasn't certain what I wanted to do. My parents wanted me to be a doctor but – well – my grades weren't good enough, so I sort of found my way into law. I think that's for the best because I can't stand blood!

Interviewer: Know what you mean, Chris.

Chris: Yeh. But I did want a professional career and law's proved interesting. So, l mean, after graduation I saw this agency job advertised and it looked really interesting and here I am.

Interviewer: Right. So, how relevant is your legal degree?

Chris: Well, I don't use my law studies directly but the background knowledge in international law has proved very important, especially in negotiations between the Canadian firms and clients in China or Japan. Often there are millions of dollars involved in these negotiations and the legal details need to be very carefully worked out. Now we do have a team of special international lawyers to do that, but it is a help if I understand the general picture.

Interviewer: Yeh, I can see that, Chris. Sure. What other skills do you need in this kind of work?

Chris: Well languages are certainly important.

Interviewer: Do you speak Japanese or Chinese?

Chris: No Chinese at all unfortunately but I did do an undergraduate course in Japanese at college and this has proved very helpful, both in social situations and I think, well, it creates a good impression with clients. It lets them know that you're interested in them and that you're trying. I speak Spanish as well because both of my parents come from Venezuela. But working in Japan and China, I don't speak Spanish very much.

Interviewer: I suppose not. No. Tell me, Chris, you've just got back from Beijing. Where to next?

Chris: Well, my next trip is to Tokyo in a couple of weeks. We're setting up a fair there to promote Canadian fashions and design. Fashion and design's a new area for me and also for the agency. Now, we know it's difficult to break into the Japanese market, so it's going to be a very big challenge for us, but I'm really excited about it.

Interviewer: Canadian fashion in Japan! Wow! How do you think that's going to go down, Chris?

Speaker: That is the end of the fourth section. You now have thirty seconds to check your answers.

You now have one minute to check all your answers.

► ANSWER KEYS

PRACTICE TEST 1: ACADEMIC MODULE

1. A. Time
   B. Place
   C. Magnitude
2. A
3. A. Howling of dogs
   B. Changes in metabolic rates
4. A
5. T
6. F
7. F
8. F
9. F
10. T
11. B
12. C
13. D
14. C
15. D
16. C
17. I
18. F
19. B
20. C
21. D
22. G
23. D
24. A
25. F
26. C
27. E
28. P
29. H
30. O
31. G
32. K
33. C
34. B
35. J
36. L

PRACTICE TEST 2: ACADEMIC MODULE

1. Lead, Cadmium, Mercury
2. F
3. F
4. T
5. T
6. B
7. D
8. F
9. A ,D
10. R
11. H
12. Q
13. O
14. J
15. T
16. K
17. A
18. L
19. S
20. C
21. M
22. E
23. N
24. D
25. P
26. F
27. H
28. B
29. A
30. C
31. D
32. C
33. B
34. A
35. A
36. B

PRACTICE TEST 3: ACADEMIC MODULE

1. G
2. A
3. H
4. J
5. C
6. F
7. A
8. K
9. M
10. 1
11. P
12. O
13. L
14. G
15. E
16. D
17. A
18. B
19. A
20. A
21. C
22. C
23. B
24. C
25. A
26. B
27. E
28. G
29. A
30. A
31. A
32. C
33. A
34. B
35. A
36. C

PRACTICE TEST 4: GENERAL TRAINING MODULE

1. B	13. A	27. switched
2. D	14. B	28. near
3. telephone 5664000	15. C	29. condition
4. her licence may be cancelled	16. C	30. fails
	17. C	31. protect
5. hand it in at any Motor Registry	18. A	32. a large burner
	19. four hours	33. A
6. the Reid Room	20. 8.00 p.m.	34. C
7. 7.00 p.m.	21. the employer	35. 10 minutes
8. 8.30 p.m.	22. C	36. A
9. 088	23. A	37. B
10. 066	24. B	38. plastic
11. 019	25. B	39. Celsius
12. 044	26. pulling	40. C

PRACTICE LISTENING TEST

Section 1

1. C

2. B

3. C

4. D

5. Crystal

6. Cheadle

7. SK8 4RT

8. British

9. August 12

10. B

11. A

Section 2

12. 895

13. Liverpool

14. 7

15. driver

16. front

17. sides

18. (signalling) light

19. 00876935

PRACTICE LISTENING TEST

Section 3

20. T
21. F
22. F
23. F
24. F
25. T
26. T
27. T
28. F

Section 4

29. Japan and China
30. negotiating
31. electronics
32. six months
33. work (catching up on paperwork, writing reports)
34. informal settings like restaurants
35. medicine/doctor
36. negotiations
37. Japanese, Spanish
38. new area/very big challenge